EVERY WAKING MOMENT

Every Waking Moment

by James Crews

LynxHousePress

Cover Art: *Morning Sun* by Arthur G. Dove; Courtesy of the Philips Collection, Washington, D.C.
Author Photo: Christy Nevius
Book Design: Taylor D. Waring | taylordwaring.com

FIRST EDTION

This and other award-winning titles may be viewed at www.lynxhousepress.com

Lynx House Press titles are distributed by the University of Washington Press (hfscustserv@press.jhu.edu).

ISBN 978-0-89924-172-2

Library of Congress Cataloging-in-Publication data may be obtained from the Library of Congress.

Contents

For Ted Kooser, who taught me to pay attention.

Only that day dawns to which we are awake.

— Henry David Thoreau

Part One

Meditation Class

I paused in the rain outside the storefront,
though there was no sign, only the image
of a lotus on the steamed-over window.
Inside, rows of people crouched on cushions,
eyes closed, their legs folded beneath them.
Some were mouthing what I took to be
a mantra, a few words in Sanskrit meant
to make them hum as one with the universe.
I wiped the fog from the glass and saw
a statue of the Buddha on a shelf, laughing
at himself, laughing at me standing there
in a puddle, under a pine tree that kept
dripping on my head, keeping perfect time
with my heartbeat. The night seemed to slow
the longer I watched those students going
nowhere and doing nothing together—
until there were no more worries about
the rent, no sick parents or ex-boyfriends.
Only a car passing by on the slick street,
the sound of something being torn in two.

The Unadorned Here and Now

It arrives when the heart is centered,
little bubble in the level that tells you
all is well for now, the rain leaking in
through rips in the screen, the spider
crawling on the bed beside your pillow,
the moth orchid you found by the road
losing its yellowing, dried-out leaves.
Let everything happen to you, Rilke wrote,
and I repeat it to myself every time
my housemate, the exiled Chinese poet
comes home, storms up the stairs,
and cracks open the first of many
beers he will drink, staying up all night
to write of past loves and the wolves
he once saw from a cabin in the snowy
mountains of Tennessee. I listen
to his footsteps and count my own
breaths, which say only *now* and *now*,
and help to calm the heart banging
in my chest, saying, *yes, this, yes, this*
and this—accept and love that pacing
man as you love the footfalls of rain,
the way ice-cold water meets the lips
with a sting.

Symphony

A gift in the form of a silent morning
on this day before Thanksgiving—
no downstairs neighbor slamming doors
or flipping on the exhaust fan
in her bathroom, no dull roar waking me.
No jackhammer ripping up the street
outside my building or workmen
shouting to each other over the noise
of dump trucks full of gravel
rattling the icy window panes.
For now, only the thunk of my knife
on the cutting board as I slice
a honeycrisp apple. Only the sound
of my own measured breathing
a lover once told me was beautiful
while we were kissing. As I slide
the pieces of apple into a bowl,
put a pot of water on the stove to boil,
I know not every day can be like this,
attention paid to every small thing—
scooping coffee into the filter,
turning the faucet that sends
hot water over the knife I'm rinsing.
But before I forget, I want to say
thank you to whatever force
gives us these moments of reprieve
like the pauses in a symphony
that cause us to listen even harder
once the music resumes.

Secret Music

I wanted to play the piano growing up,
but there was no money for lessons
and no one who could teach me,
so my parents bought a toy piano—
a plinking, tuneless thing that made
a music awful to the ears. For years,
an ache stretched to my fingertips
and stayed: nothing could take it away.
And though I don't remember the day
someone showed me how to shape
the letters of my name, I can still feel
the pencil's beveled edges resting against
my thumb, which came together with
the other fingers almost at the point
to aim the lead at the lined paper
laid before me. The muscles and bones
of my hand already sensing the notes
of a secret music hidden in words.

Deus Humanus

We are gods who are also human.
Each a divine being who reaches
into murky gray dishwater, through
the orange scrim of swirling grease
to wash the last saucepan before bed.
I don't know what to call the force
that flows through our veins, makes us
a conduit for flashes of insight, jolts
of knowing there are no borders
between us. But I know the names
of neighborhoods, can read the color-
coded maps of subway systems.
I can insert my card in a machine,
take the twenty-dollar bill it spits out
and buy a lunch of cold noodles
with sesame, scallions and broccoli,
which I know how to spear with
the tines of my plastic fork. I can sit
on a bench outside the cathedral
and eat while pigeons swoop between
steeples, landing on the concrete
at my feet, and looking up at me
like a deity they can't help but disdain
as they beg for crumbs.

Morning Commute

I know I'm awake by the grace
of whatever makes it so.
The bedside lamp throws
its glow across the carpet,
lighting my rented room
on the top floor of a building
from which I can see
the red buds of sugar maples
whose wood, a friend told me,
burns brightest in winter,
making a happy flame
that dances in the fireplace
and laughs itself alive
with each crackle and spark.
No fire for me today
as I make my way to the train
with a cup of coffee
warming the bare hand
that brings it to my lips
so I can keep kissing
this morning hello, wishing
that the silence of these
sleeping row houses
and rain-slick sidewalks
might never end. Before going
into the station, I stop
and take a photo of the sun
like a smoldering coal
burning through clouds

banked above a block
of condos whose windows
have all turned to gold.

Daylight Saving, Age Five

The night my mother turned back the clocks
I thought that while we slept the hours stolen
from everyone on earth would collect like coins
in a bank vault, so we'd wake up rich at last.
Even as my mother explained that it meant
only extra dreams in winter, only late light
returned to us with daffodils and rain in spring,
I was cupping my hands under every lamp,
keeping the fridge open, so the cold brightness
would pool at my feet. *Honey*, she said, *it doesn't
work like that.* But I didn't listen. I was seeing
daylight leaking slowly from the dripping comb
of the sun and into bowls, jars, and bottles—
anything with a lid I placed on the window sills
to gather the sweet morning light I wanted
to smear on slices of bread, eat with a spoon.

Before School

I sat alone in the daybreak kitchen,
my mother having placed on the table
two pieces of nearly burnt toast
smeared with butter and grape jelly
melting together in my mouth
with each new bite, sweet into cream,
and becoming the taste of a time
before thinking and secrets and lies—
of freedom. The whole house hummed
around me, almost silent before
my brother woke to Looney Tunes
on the console TV, before trash trucks
and buses rumbled along the streets.
For a moment, only the intermittent
tick and sigh of the coffeemaker
heating the glass carafe of Folgers.
Only my mother swishing by
in her nightgown, then leaning toward
the flame on the stove to light
the day's first cigarette—slight sizzle
of paper and tobacco as she sucked in,
exhaled the smoke I could have sworn
I smelled today when I slid bread
into the toaster, and the coils inside
began to glow.

Waiting for the Subway

When I step from the stuttering escalator
onto the platform, a shaft of sun
slants down from windows in the station,
shining on the faces of passengers so they
have to squint as they stare into the tunnel,
waiting for the blinking eyes of a late
blue line train to arrive. And as I pass
from darkness into that dawn, a shiver runs
the length of my spine, and I remember
how I used to play with my mother's hair—
scent of vanilla as I lifted it gingerly
from her neck, then tied it in a ponytail
with a rubber band. How she would shudder
and rub the goose bumps on her arms, saying
Someone must've walked over my grave today.

After Surgery

My mother was still getting dressed
when I stepped into the room.
She moved gently, wincing even
as she fumbled with the buttons
on her blouse. But her face lit up
when she saw me come to take her
home: *There's my baby*, she whispered,
then asked if I could help put on
her socks and shoes. As I knelt,
coaxing the white cotton over her
delicate ankles, a wave of grief
passed through me, for the son
I once was and never would be again.
I had to grip one of the chair legs
just to keep myself steady, and then
I did what was asked, easing her feet
into sneakers and tying the laces
in double-knots so they might never
come undone.

The Beginning of the World

I hear the howling wind as I hear my mother
sighing in the next room, perched on the edge
of the mattress because she can't move
her legs tonight. Soon I'll go to her, pry
the white roses of used tissues from each hand
and ease her into bed. But for now, I listen
to footfalls of raindrops making their way across
the tin roof, and imagine the first downpour
that startled our world into being, filling a puddle
with water enough for a single-celled creature
to swim around in, until the shimmering instant
it decided to climb out, took a breath, then split
into two, giving birth to another just like it
in the mud, begging to be held. By the time
I open the door to my mother's bedroom,
she's fast asleep, chin resting on her chest.
I peel back the sheets and blanket, gather her
as best I can into my arms, and tuck her in
so tenderly, she doesn't even know I'm here.

This Time

This time, I'd take my mother's hand
as she stepped into the viewing room,
my father lying with fingers intertwined
in the casket no one told me would be open.
This time, I'd keep her from stumbling
on the burgundy carpet, and I'd be
what she reached for to steady herself,
instead of an empty chair. And when she
nearly fell upon seeing him there like that,
giving a yelp as if her leg had been caught
in a trap, I'd know my parents were
more in love than I'd ever imagined.
If I could go back now, I'd arc an arm
against the small of her back, and become
the husband for a moment, our grief
a single thing slung across our shoulders,
two buckets swinging on either side,
almost too heavy to bear as we approach
the open casket, each of us now
holding one of his hands.

My Mother's Visitation

When she starts coughing
then goes suddenly silent,
I rush into the living room
where she sleeps in her recliner,
and watch until she draws
a few deep breaths, helped by
the plastic tubes inserted
in her nose, the oxygen pump
whirring in the corner.
She begins snoring again,
and I go back to bed, but can't
stop seeing her mouth
gone slack, open wide—
as if she had seen something
astounding in her dream.
Perhaps my father, the man
she hasn't touched in years,
came back, his bearded face
flashing blue in the TV's
mute glow as he whispered
her name, then leaned over
the chair and kissed her
one last time, leaving behind
only a whiff of his warm,
tobacco-scented breath
so she would know it was him,
so that for a moment they were
breathing the same air.

Telling My Mother

We sat on the sagging side porch of her trailer
smoking cigarettes in that sudden stillness
after supper, when time no longer exists.
In the creek behind us, something splashed
while above, the ice chips of stars glinted,
their edges growing sharper in the coming dark.
Though she had not asked and would never
ask about it, though there was no snapshot
of a smiling man I could point to and say,
Look, I love him, I have always been this way—
I told her. And in the silence that followed,
I turned to watch the tiger lilies rustling
against the shed like spent torches, their sun-
scorched and shriveled petals now ready
to fall apart. My mother looked hard at me
as if to memorize every feature of my face.
Honey, she said, *I already knew*, then blew smoke
from the side of her mouth, bluish tendrils
that clung to the air between us.

Letter to a Future Lover

This is just to tell you
whoever you are, wherever you are
I don't mind sitting here
alone in this room going dark,
watching the sky outside turn slowly
pink and the sun sinking
like a coin in its slot of horizon.

I don't mind waiting
for you to walk into the room
where I've been listening for years
for footsteps on the worn carpet,
for the sudden scrape
of the tarnished brass doorknob
as it turns, and then
the disturbance that is the heat
and rhythm of another
body moving closer.

I now know I cannot know
when you'll arrive, and so
I must live on the scraps of fantasy
until that moment when you
approach from behind
at the folding card table where I write
by the gauzy light of a lamp
I have at last snapped on,
slipping these words into
the envelope of the present moment
and sending them on to you.

Note to Self

When no one's called in days,
go inside. Sit beside the box fan
and watch the blades spinning
inside their plastic cage, giving air.
Take the time to notice how
your slow-growing coral cactus
has sprouted what seems to be
the nub of a new arm ridged
with tiny pink blossoms that
reach for the feast of summer light.
Pour water onto its bed of sun-
warmed gravel and understand
you've been sent here to pay
attention even when it seems
there's no reward beyond this
fleeting sense that someone else
out there is listening.

Lesser Prayer

Tired of sirens, the slamming of car doors
and stomping of students in the flat below,
I beg of the air: Please, let there be less.
I ask the god in me who's as peaceful
as the ten-foot wooden Buddha I once saw
sitting lotus in his own room at a museum:
Give me room to breathe and the silence
of a city street at 4am, blacktop bathed
in the glow of a streetlamp haloed by fog
lifting off snowbanks taller than I am.
Take back the blue light thrown off
by our screens, each one a false dawn,
and give everyone their own earbuds
so I can hear the real world again—
pneumatic huff of subway doors forced
open and shut, squeak of my boots
crossing new snow laid over concrete
like a prayer mat. Be like that, Lord—
a series of interlocking flakes that fall
wherever we step, and make us look up,
take our time. Be sleet, be power outage,
let life become an eternal snow day
so I can stay home if I want, with only
the buzz of a lamp, tick of the fridge,
creak of the carpeted floor as I take my cup
of coffee and sit by the window, watching
the contents of someone's trash bin
blow silently down the snow-lined street.

Winter Morning

When I can no longer say thank you
for this new day and the waking into it,
for the cold scrape of the kitchen chair
and the ticking of the space heater turning
orange as it warms the floor near my feet,
I know it is because I've been fooled again
by the selfish, unruly man who lives in me
and believes he deserves only safety
and comfort. But if I pause as I do now,
and watch the streetlights outside winking
off one by one like old men closing their
cloudy eyes, if I listen to my tired neighbors
slamming car doors hard against the morning
and see the steaming coffee in their mugs
kissing their chapped lips as they sip and
exhale each of their worries white into
the icy air around their faces—then I can
remember this one life is a gift each of us
was handed and told to open: Untie the bow
and tear off the paper, look inside
and be grateful for whatever you find
even if it is only the scent of a tangerine
that lingers on the fingers long after
you've finished eating it.

The Gift

The man shuffled onto the subway
wearing paint-spattered overalls
and holding a plastic water bottle
from the mouth of which climbed
the cutting of a spider plant.
He pressed it to his chest as we
rattled through soot-black tunnels
whose walls wept like catacombs,
the automatic doors letting in ghosts
of smoke and exhaust each time
they forced themselves open and shut.
We all covered our noses and mouths,
shook our heads, but the man kept
looking down at that living thing
in his hands and grinning, rubbing
its leaves as if he could feel the plant
breathing our leftover breath.

At Back Bay Station

It Never Hurts To Be Alert, the signs
posted in the train station remind us,
but it does strain us to look up
from the blue-lit screens of our phones
and really see the weary faces
of others on their way elsewhere.
It's hard to hear the noise pouring out
of earbuds, to watch the hurried woman
with a stroller and twin daughters
whose matching red ribbons hang loose
in their tousled hair as they sprint
from one end of the station to the other,
their mother stopping to wipe what appears
to be tears from the corner of her eye.
It takes patience to walk downstairs
when it's time, the breathless train already
rumbling into the tunnel—to take one
step at a time and feel the ridges
in the rubber runners bolted down so we
won't slip, to notice the worn edges
where countless passengers have passed
before, lost in thought, each of us
running an absent hand along the smooth
oak banister as we plan away our days.

Part Two

A Reckoning

How many times have I failed
to watch the pink of sunrise-light
fade from a field of clouds in a sky
no one has ever seen before
from this place on the earth in the middle
of a lucky country, far from the din
of wars drowning out the sound
of bells calling the hour of prayer?

How could I not have noticed
the glass of water on my nightstand
with its countless bubbles of air
containing a bit of the expelled breath
of everything alive and dead on the planet,
waiting to become part of me?

How many nights did I not feel
the links in the chain of the bedside lamp
as I pulled the wool of darkness
closer around me, and how could I
have neglected to keep my eyes open
to the flashes of passing headlights
sweeping across the walls of the room
as if searching for something lost?

Bedroom

It's so quiet I can hear a moth
caught in the space
between window and curtain—

flitting back and forth and leaving
trails of rubbed-off scales
on the cloth and glass.

The moth and I both restless,
both longing to be free.

To Change

Then came the rainy day
at the height of summer
in the middle of my life
when I knew I would have to
build an altar to change.
No mudslide had toppled
the house, no trees fallen
to block the roads out of town—
I simply woke to the sound
of rain on the driveway,
saw a curtain of it falling
in front of my open window
and a small puddle forming
on the hardwood floor.
I dipped my toes into
the cold water, and without
even a shiver understood
that change was the only
god I could ever worship.
No bells rang out, no peal
of thunder rumbled the room,
announcing my revelation.
The rain just kept on
slicking the concrete, falling
on the scorched grass
and making it seem greener
in the grayish first light.

Holy Sonnet: Spring
after John Donne

In rain-battered flowerbeds, petals blown
from tulip-heads, like ticket stubs, lift and rise
on biting wind. But the day is lit by infinities
of giggling grade-schoolers boarding a bus to go
to warm, open classrooms, not yet overthrown
by detention or heroin, by the droning tyrannies
of chemistry and algebra, the nickel-dull eyes
of the terrorist on today's front page. No woe
stains their fingers like ink, no thoughts of space
expanding, or the planet to which we're bound
burning up. They are happy, a sudden grace
filling the bus that rumbles by, the wet ground
now spongy, free of frost, giving way to good
grass sprouting again in mud as thick as blood.

No Answers

All day, the eyes of the mass shooter
stayed with me, his life an equation
none of us could solve. And the news
like a ravenous hawk kept plunging
into the hours I'd rather have spent
chopping carrots for curry soup
or clearing cobwebs from light fixtures—
measuring the distance between each
sunstruck strand of woven silk.

But how to reckon the distance between
my history and his, or add what he did
to the list of ills we must face each day?
His blank face was the merlin perched
on the fencepost this morning, feasting
on a sparrow snatched mid-flight, headed
to the feeder I'd just filled—feathers
tossed pell-mell into the wind until
there were too many to count.

What Salt Does

I sprinkle salt
on slices of eggplant
to draw out the bitter juices,
the excess water
hidden inside skin the color
of an elaborate bruise
months from healing.
Then I let them rest on a towel
until it's time
to wipe away the beads of moisture
as one dabs at the eyes—
grief finally brought to the surface,
but still too fresh to speak.

After Work

When I passed his bedroom, my father
looked up from the grease-stained T-shirt
his cheek was resting on, and asked me
for a massage. I don't know how it became
our thing, why he claimed only my hands
could unknot his muscles after a double
shift at the plastics factory. But that day,
as he reached around and rubbed his back
where it hurt the most, I just stood there
watching the jaundiced late light leak in
through drawn blinds, asking him if this
could wait till later. And when he nodded,
said it was no big deal, I turned away
from his pleading, blue-gray eyes, back to
the laugh-track of some sitcom I loved,
thinking I knew what love was.

The Pool

Because he couldn't afford
the kidney-shaped, in-ground pool
we all wanted, my father went out
and bought a used galvanized pool
whose rusted rim I refused to touch.

As usual, he found a solution,
and split a length of black rubber hose
down the middle with his pocketknife
then stretched it over the rough sides,
inch by inch, until no rust showed.

Back then, I never thought such gestures
were selfless, evidence of what we call
unconditional love. But now I feel
my small hands gripping soft rubber,
and I see my father on the back porch,

cigarette hanging from his smiling lips
as he watches me lift myself
out of the pool, flinging cold water
from my goose-pimpled skin
as if I'd been reborn again.

Visitation from My Father

Was that you today, busking downtown,
flashing your few good teeth, eyes shining
like dimes as you strummed a ukulele,
case splayed on the sidewalk in filthy snow?

Was that you who saw the pause in my eyes,
who knew I'd stop before I did, who said,
Finally, a man with a heart! as I dropped two
dollar bills into the worn, velvet-lined case?

Was that your voice saying, *Come here*, as you
pocketed the money, holding out your arms
so I had no choice but to let you embrace me
on the street as businessmen lined up for lunch?

I patted your dusty back, ready to catch my bus,
but it was just like life: you wouldn't let me go
until you'd pressed each of your stubbled cheeks
against mine, warmth passed from man to man.

All I Want

Two decades without him, and all I want
is one of my father's plain white T-shirts
draped over the back of a chair after work,
to trace the map of grease-stains and islands
leftover from his dried-out sweat.

To feel it peeling off his back as he asks
for another massage, and to give it this time
with full knowledge of how much pain he's in,
without counting down the minutes
on his bedside clock.
                          To see that jade cross
dangling beneath the band of his V-neck
as he bends to tend the tomatoes, to ask
why he dug it out of a flea market box,
and started wearing it those last months,
rubbing the stone when he thought
no one was looking.
                          To lift one of his T-shirts
out of the closet where I keep them, and feel
my hand reaching through the cotton weave
to work the knots from his aching back
one last time.

Don't

It can be a kind of in-the-moment prayer
you say under your breath as you
watch the tired mother raise her hand,
about to hit her crying toddler
gripping a candy bar in the checkout.

Or when you pass a handsome man
on the street as he stops to fumble
with the pack in his pocket, lifting out
a cigarette, which he lets hang
from full lips as he digs for a lighter—

Don't, you whisper. But it can be said
without speaking, like the time
I tried to cross Broadway against the light,
and an elderly woman on the other side
widened her eyes, a hand flying up

to her stricken mouth. I stopped just as
a Camaro barreled by out of nowhere—
her face telling me, *Don't move*,
and we both stood stock-still, breathless
with gratitude for what I didn't do.

You Never Know

You never know if what you're doing,
no matter how slight it seems,
might be saving someone's life.

It could be letting the woman cut
in front of you on the crowded freeway
with a flick of the wrist wave,

or the extra few minutes you take
alone in your car one day that makes
the space that allows you to smile

at the man standing behind you
in line at the coffee shop. Maybe
he scrawls his name and number

on the back of a crumpled receipt
and slips it to you folded
into a neat square. And maybe

coming home from work that night
you remember that number in your pocket
and feel the flutter and swoop

of hope in your chest again
like the lone monarch butterfly
gliding through the darkening yard.

Part Three

Through the Gates

I turned off the state highway
and drove up his rutted lane,
through the narrow gates
he left propped open for me.
Gravel snapped beneath my tires,
ticking in the undercarriage
as he stepped out of the house.

The fog they call holy smoke
hung over the mountains,
and crows cawed from bare trees
to welcome me, holding their vigil
for the vanishing daylight.

Some truths arrive plainer
to the waiting mind and shock us
awake. I said this to myself
on the way to see him: You must
put yourself in the path of joy
to find it—you must be willing
to let your heart get battered
and bruised by disappointment.

But for once, it wasn't. Love came
rushing at me like a gust of wind
as when someone you sense
you have always known
opens his arms and holds you close.

Finding Love Again After Years

is like coming upon a moth-orchid
half-dead by the side of the street,
set out with the bags of last week's trash.

You rescue and nourish it, tell yourself
you'd be happy even if it never bloomed—
leaves gleaming a glossy green,

the insistent arms of aerial roots
reaching up from their bed of woodchips
to sip the humid air. *These are enough*

of beauty for me, you think. But then
a cluster of tight buds appears at the tip
of a stem in need of propping up, and one

of the blossoms pops open overnight,
flashing its white and pink-veined wings
like a revelation of all the pleasure

you've been missing for years.

No Borders

Pollen swirled on top of the water
as sunlight flashed on the stone walls
of the small cove we slipped into,
escaping the last of the August heat.
The cold water numbed my body,
and that initial surrender to the shiver
that coursed through me, then hovered
above my skin for the rest of the day
was practice for every future moment
of giving in, like walking with your hands
turned outward, how the belly relaxes
and your breathing eases as you move
in a pose of total exposure.

This is not the life I once imagined—
living not just in a small town
but on the outskirts of it, far away
from coffee shops and supermarkets,
close to sugar maples, goldenrod,
and the ragged, almost blown-apart
doilies of Queen Anne's Lace
sprouting at the edges of fields.

They are letting go as I have let go
into this new life, giving myself over
to the man who leads me deeper
and deeper into the quieting woods,
who's taught me the pleasure
of wading into a river, then going
under again and again until there are
no borders between body and water,
between past and present moment.

Sleepless Stars

I get up one last time and look out
at the tired lights still blinking
in the blackness beyond our window,
and for a moment, I think I see
a constellation breaking free of sky,
climbing higher, but then notice
wingtips and contrails and imagine
the captain dimming the cabin
as restless passengers reach up
to turn on their reading lamps,
each one bringing their own star to life
in the tight, dark space above them.
For the rest of the night, they'll fly
through clouds like minor gods
while down here, I watch you
thrashing in dreams I'll never know—
no matter. I ease into bed, sliding
by instinct onto the warm, moonlit
strip of sheet beside you.

Meditation

I am this bare sugar maple
swaying in gusts of wind,
tossed about by the storm
of my own thundering thoughts.

But I am learning just to breathe,
inhaling the loamy scent of spring
and the stench of a dead mouse
slowly decaying somewhere in the yard.

And I am exhaling the purified air
others will take into their lungs,
chests expanding and contracting
with trace amounts of me.

Let the points of my attention be
like leaves unfurling from the wicks
of buds on branch-tips ready to blaze
with a fire that burns cleaner

and greener than any other kind.

Thinking

I have trained myself to say
thinking to myself each time I feel
my thoughts straining at their leash,
about to become a pack of coyotes
combing the night of my mind
and yipping like drunks when they find
some easy prey to gnaw on
till sunrise.

But I'm not sure that saying *thinking*
makes me think any less, since now
I'm sitting on a log in a field thinking
about how much I say *thinking* to myself
when I should be kneeling at the feet
of stalks of goldenrod leaning
toward the ground after last night's rain
and weary of the feast of light and heat
at summer's end.

I should be as industrious as the bees,
streaks of pollen dusting my cheeks,
caked like mud on feet and wings.
Or as watchful as the sparrowhawk
hovering a hundred feet above
with ultraviolet eyes tracing
a trail of urine left in the grass
by a fleeing vole.

I want to be as devout as that vole,
saying the rosary with clicking seeds
and praying that dried-out ragweed
will be enough to conceal
the hole he and his loved ones live in,
huddled close and shivering
as a wide-winged shadow passes
over their heads.

From an Amtrak Along the Hudson

I saw a bald eagle perched on a log,
the beacon of his white head alerting me
to his presence in the estuary
where he stood with the writhing
silver body of a fish gripped tight
in talons that would not release
until his catch had exhausted itself.
He watched from a distance, undisturbed
as a much larger silver body slid by
on the tracks, and he seemed
to meet my gaze for an instant—
both of us hunting in our own ways
for something bright to bring home.

At a Cafe in Montréal

To escape the blast of blowing sleet,
I take the only available seat
by a bank of steamed-over windows
no one can see out of except
through a few small patches where
the heart-shaped leaves of this
potted oxalis, also known
as the purple love plant, have breathed
against the glass, erasing the steam
so that a little of the weak
winter light might leak in today
and feed us all.

Komorebi

I'm sitting at a table in a cafe,
taking in the *komorebi*, Japanese word
for the play of light through leaves—
the dance of it on the floor, my shirt,
across the faux-wood surface
of the table on which my latte rests.
Can we have a word in English
for that excitable light, some way
to say I'm grateful for the boredom
of this summer day because it lets
space bloom in the mind where
nothing else needs to be stored?
Can we have a word for coffee-
when-I-don't-need-it, indulgence
without the guilt, eating and drinking
something just for the taste of it—
like the pint of strawberries
I polished off this morning before
leaving the house: sweet crush
in the mouth like the first lines
of a song you know by heart,
or how just saying a lover's name
brings back the sensation of teeth
on your neck on his king-size bed.
There should be a word for sex-
in-the-afternoon—something more

sacred than *quickie*, something more
needful than *delight* that includes
each playful bite but also the shifting
glance of sun through the skylight
blessing each of your sweaty bodies after.

Relish

There is no difference
between *relish* and *release*
since what pleases us
frees us, if we can
pay enough attention—

scent of a chicken roasting
in the slow-cooker,
water beaded on the glass lid,

and the tarp over the woodpile
whipping in autumn wind,
rippling and crackling
with anticipation
of all the fires to come.

Then there is the absence
that is also pleasure—
the silent phone
whose screen stays black,
so the day becomes
like an empty bowl
scrubbed out and placed
on the dish drain,
the kitchen so quiet now
I can hear every drop of water
leaking from the faucet.

Picking Strawberries in Rain
for Anthony Ray Hinton

Daylight strains through storm clouds
just after dawn, and as I walk down
to the fields, a gentle rain touches
the sides of my face, tender as a mother
who hasn't seen me in months. I kneel
on beds of wet straw, searching for
flashes of deep red among the leaves,
and think of that man from Alabama
kept on death row for thirty years
for a crime he didn't commit. The dust
wiped off the gun they said he used.
How he said all he wanted, once
released, was to feel the sun shining
on his face again—and rain, the purest
thing, because *it came from God*. I lift
the ripest berry to my lips and bite
into it, thinking now: If I am ever
locked away, this is the freedom
I'll crave each day: juice running
down my chin, staining my fingers
as I pick and eat, pick and eat
these strawberries made colder
and sweeter by rain in the night.

How They Come Back

The dead return to us when it rains.
They surround our houses with the sound
of their footsteps crossing the grass,
then tap at windows behind which
we have been biding our time.

They make us throw off blankets, rise
from quiet beds and open our doors
to this staccato they have practiced
for weeks in the soundproof rooms
of storm clouds that finally released them.

They need us to look at streetlights
and see the shadowed, shattered pieces
of their souls falling back to earth
to touch again the wind chimes, lawn chairs
and parked cars they never loved enough in life.

And when we step into the yard, we let
the familiar arms of fog wrap around us
as our cheeks streak with what we think
must be only water that grew too heavy
and cold for the sky to hold.

Into the Mystery

Push into the mystery
instead of against it.
See through each new day
as if you stand at the end
of a long hallway,
not knowing where it leads.
See faces. Trace outlines
of bodies you've never
encountered as my husband
did earlier today, saying
that out of the corner
of his eye, even though
he'd never met him,
he saw my late father
standing for a moment
among the tight rows
of tasseled-out sweet corn
backlit by slanting rays
of afternoon sun. I believe
in visions and visitations,
and trust that it was
actually my father
who came to me once
in a dream, asking
how I knew he was
always with me, then
opening his arms when I
gave him the only answer
I could: *I just do*.

Drala

The mind craves a safe place,
some space of relief to look forward to—
a few hours before work, the plush chair
whose cushion cups your weight exactly.

We must find a way to live in
each instant of what the Tibetans call
drala—dazzle and magic of the everyday—
which translates as *above or beyond the enemy*.

If I could, I'd build my house
out of the sound of gathering rain
I heard today, cascade of droplets
that swooped down slow, dismantling

the silence as I sat by an open window
listening to the notes of that primordial song
which has been the same for centuries—
rain in the trees, rain slicking each stone.

I'm carving a door in my mind to slip through
when I need to remember that *drala*
is always with me, whether I'm drinking
a cup of green tea or washing my hair

or rubbing lotion into my hands and elbows.
Every motion I pay total attention to
becomes a retreat not away from life
but deeper into it, even when the phone

won't stop ringing, and my screens keep
beaming their bad news back to me.
All I have to do is sit still and listen,
let rain take my hand and guide me inside.

The Given Moment

When I laid my head
on your shoulder
and breathed in
the heat of the dryer
and lavender scent
of laundry detergent
still embedded in
the shirt you put on
before bed, I knew
I'd always remember
that moment given
to each of us, even
when the crows-feet
creasing our eyes
have deepened into
ravines, even when
this head I rest
on your chest
has gone as soft
and white as wisps
of milkweed spilling
into autumn wind.

Post and Beam

I asked him if they were meant
to split like that, meaning the beams
holding up our ceiling, and he said yes,
cracks—or *checks*, as they're known—
are normal in all timber frame homes
as posts and beams begin to dry out.
Still, when I heard the house popping
those first nights and leaped out of bed,
thinking gunshot or shattered window,
I wondered how cracked pine could
make for a sounder structure that only
grows stronger, more solid with time.
Yet I must have known even then
that love breaks us the same as we
bend and swell and learn to settle,
inseparable, into each other.

Acknowledgments

The author wishes to thank the Vermont Community Foundation for a generous Creation Grant from the Vermont Arts Endowment Fund, which made the writing of this book possible. I am also indebted to David Axelrod, Jodi Varon, and Christopher Howell, all of whom believed in this book and saw it into the world.

Poems from this collection have been published, sometimes in slightly different form, in the following magazines and journals:

"The Unadorned Here and Now" in *December*;
"Meditation Class" in *Southern Poetry Review*;
"Secret Music" in *Balkan Press*;
"Daylight Saving, Age Five" in *The MacGuffin*;
"Waiting for the Subway" in *Alexandria Review*;
"This Time" in *Tiferet*;
"My Mother's Visitation" in *Communion Arts Magazine* (Australia);
"Telling My Mother" in *Nimrod International Journal*;
"All I Want" as "This Time" in *North Dakota Quarterly*;
"At Back Bay Station," "Don't," "Thinking," and "Post and Beam"
        in *The Wayfarer*;
"From a Train Along the Hudson" in *New York by Rail Magazine*;
"Picking Strawberries in Rain" in *Pinyon*;
"At a Cafe in Montreal" in *Third Wednesday*;
"How They Come Back" in *basalt magazine*.

The author also wishes to thank the following for their ongoing support: Megan Mayhew Bergman and The Robert Frost Stone House at Bennington College, the Eastern Oregon University MFA program, Tracy Davies, Dafydd Wood, and Chris Morrow at the Northshire Bookstore, Jennie Rozycki and the John G. McCullough Free Library, Kristi Nelson, Katie Rubinstein, Br. David Steindl-Rast, and everyone at A Network for Grateful Living, and Dede Cummings, the dedicated staff of Green Writers Press, and Jenna Gersie at The Hopper. I'm also indebted to the many students who have attended my Mindfulness and Writing workshops over the years, including Ellen Perry Berkeley, Amy Bremel, Anna Chapman, Carol Cone, Alice Gilborn, Ray Hudson, Heather Newman, Mary Ellen Rudolph, and Peggy Verdi: you have all taught me far more than I could ever teach you.

Gratitude to the many friends, teachers, and colleagues whose support and encouragement made me a better poet over the years: David Axelrod, Grace Bauer, Jennifer Boyden, Megan Buchanan, David Clewell (who started it all), Dede Cummings, Todd Davis, Chard deNiord, Pat Emile, Laura Foley, Patricia Fontaine, Margaret Hasse, Kim Hays, Jane Hirshfield, Christopher Howell, Anne Hunter, Mary Elder Jacoben, Jesse Lee Kercheval, Samantha Kolber, Ted Kooser, Megan Kruse, Rachel Michaud, Judy Mitchell, Travis Mossotti, Stella Nelson, Amanda Noska, Naomi Shihab Nye, Erin Quick, David Romtvedt, Marge Saiser, Julia Shipley, Shari Stenberg, Heather Swan, Sam Temple, Ross Thurber, Jodi Varon, Ron Wallace, Michael Walsh, Connie Wanek, Michelle Wiegers, and Diana Whitney. Last but not least, I thank my Peacock and Crews families, and my husband, Brad Peacock, who helps me stay awake to every given moment.

About James Crews

James Crews' work has appeared in *Ploughshares, Christian Century, The New Republic,* and *Crab Orchard Review,* among other journals, and he is a regular contributor to *The Times Literary Supplement.* His first collection of poetry, *The Book of What Stays,* won the 2010 Prairie Schooner Book Prize and received a Foreword Magazine Book of the Year Citation. He is also the author of *Telling My Father,* winner of the Cowles Poetry Prize, and editor of ***Healing the Divide: Poems of Kindness and Connection***, published by Green Writers Press. He holds an MFA in Creative Writing-Poetry from the University of Wisconsin-Madison and a PhD in Creative Writing from the University of Nebraska-Lincoln, where he was an Othmer Fellow and worked for Ted Kooser's American Life in Poetry newspaper column. He lives on part of an organic farm with his husband in Vermont and teaches in the low-residency MFA program at Eastern Oregon University. You can also find him at www.jamescrews.net.